# Hamlet

## William Shakespeare

# Hamlet

## William Shakespeare

Abridged and adapted by Emily Hutchinson

Illustrated by Steve Moore

A PACEMAKER CLASSIC

**GLOBE FEARON**
EDUCATIONAL PUBLISHER

A Division of Simon & Schuster
Upper Saddle River, New Jersey

**Executive Editor:** Joan Carrafiello
**Project Editor:** Karen Bernhaut
**Editorial Assistant:** Keisha Carter
**Production Director:** Penny Gibson
**Print Buyer:** Cheryl Johnson
**Production Editor:** Alan Dalgleish
**Desktop Specialist:** Margarita T. Linnartz
**Art Direction:** Joan Jacobus
**Marketing Manager:** Marge Curson
**Cover and Interior Illustrations:** Steve Moore
**Cover Design:** Margarita T. Linnartz

Printed in the United States of America
1 2 3 4 5 6 7 8 9 10    99 98 97 96 95

ISBN 0-835-91224-8

GLOBE FEARON EDUCATIONAL PUBLISHER
A Division of Simon & Schuster
Upper Saddle River, New Jersey

# Contents

**Act 1** . . . . . . . . . . . . . . . . . . . . . . . . . . . . . 1
   Scene 1 . . . . . . . . . . . . . . . . . . . . . . . . . . 1
   Scene 2 . . . . . . . . . . . . . . . . . . . . . . . . . 4
   Scene 3 . . . . . . . . . . . . . . . . . . . . . . . . 10
   Scene 4 . . . . . . . . . . . . . . . . . . . . . . . . 12
   Scene 5 . . . . . . . . . . . . . . . . . . . . . . . . 15

**Act 2** . . . . . . . . . . . . . . . . . . . . . . . . . . . . 19
   Scene 1 . . . . . . . . . . . . . . . . . . . . . . . . 19
   Scene 2 . . . . . . . . . . . . . . . . . . . . . . . . 22

**Act 3** . . . . . . . . . . . . . . . . . . . . . . . . . . . . 36
   Scene 1 . . . . . . . . . . . . . . . . . . . . . . . . 36
   Scene 2 . . . . . . . . . . . . . . . . . . . . . . . . 41
   Scene 3 . . . . . . . . . . . . . . . . . . . . . . . . 49
   Scene 4 . . . . . . . . . . . . . . . . . . . . . . . . 51

**Act 4** . . . . . . . . . . . . . . . . . . . . . . . . . . . . 56
   Scene 1 . . . . . . . . . . . . . . . . . . . . . . . . 56
   Scene 2 . . . . . . . . . . . . . . . . . . . . . . . . 57
   Scene 3 . . . . . . . . . . . . . . . . . . . . . . . . 58
   Scene 4 . . . . . . . . . . . . . . . . . . . . . . . . 59
   Scene 5 . . . . . . . . . . . . . . . . . . . . . . . . 61
   Scene 6 . . . . . . . . . . . . . . . . . . . . . . . . 65
   Scene 7 . . . . . . . . . . . . . . . . . . . . . . . . 66

**Act 5** . . . . . . . . . . . . . . . . . . . . . . . . . . . . 71
   Scene 1 . . . . . . . . . . . . . . . . . . . . . . . . 71
   Scene 2 . . . . . . . . . . . . . . . . . . . . . . . . 78

# Cast of Characters

| | |
|---|---|
| HAMLET | Prince of Denmark and the only child of the dead King Hamlet |
| CLAUDIUS | King of Denmark and Hamlet's uncle |
| GERTRUDE | Queen of Denmark and Hamlet's mother |
| POLONIUS | The lord chamberlain and chief adviser to Claudius |
| HORATIO | A fellow student and loyal friend of Hamlet |
| LAERTES | The son of Polonius and the brother of Ophelia |
| OPHELIA | The daughter of Polonius and sister of Laertes |
| ROSENCRANTZ AND GUILDENSTERN | Former schoolmates and friends of Hamlet |
| FORTINBRAS | The brave prince of Norway |
| VOLTEMAND AND CORNELIUS | Danish courtiers who are sent as ambassadors to Norway |
| MARCELLUS, BARNARDO, AND FRANCISCO | Guards at the castle of Elsinore |
| REYNALDO | A young man sent by Polonius to observe Laertes |

# Act 1

*King Hamlet of Denmark is dead. The ghost of King Hamlet appears to soldiers outside Elsinore, the castle. Inside the castle, Prince Hamlet's mother, Gertrude, and her new husband, King Claudius, talk to Hamlet. They tell him it is time that he stop mourning his father's death.*

*Later, King Hamlet's ghost appears and tells Prince Hamlet that he has been murdered by Claudius, his own brother. Prince Hamlet promises to get revenge for his father's murder.*

## Scene 1

*Outside Elsinore Castle in Denmark.* FRANCISCO *stands guard.* BARNARDO *enters.*

BARNARDO: It is midnight, Francisco.
    I'll take over your watch.

FRANCISCO: Many thanks for coming.
    It is bitter cold, and I am sick at heart.

BARNARDO: Has it been quiet tonight?

FRANCISCO: Extremely so.

BARNARDO: Well, good night. If you see
    The other guards, Horatio and Marcellus,
    Please tell them to hurry.

FRANCISCO: I think I hear them coming.

(HORATIO *and* MARCELLUS *enter as* FRANCISCO *exits.*)

MARCELLUS: Hello, Barnardo!

HORATIO: We'll stand watch with you.
    Has your ghost appeared again tonight?

BARNARDO: I have seen nothing.

MARCELLUS: Horatio says we imagine it.
　　He will not believe that we saw it twice.
　　That's why he came to join us tonight.
　　If the ghost appears again,
　　Horatio can see it for himself.

HORATIO: Really, now! It won't appear.

BARNARDO: Sit down awhile.
　　I'll tell the story once more.
　　Last night, when that bright star
　　Had moved to where it is now,
　　The clock struck one—

(*The* GHOST *enters.*)

MARCELLUS: Sh! Stop talking! Look—
　　Here it comes again.

BARNARDO: It looks like the dead king!

MARCELLUS: Speak to it, Horatio!

HORATIO: Who are you?
　　Why do you appear this time of night,
　　Dressed in the armor that good
　　King Hamlet used to wear? Answer me!

(*The* GHOST *exits.*)

MARCELLUS: It's gone and will not answer.

BARNARDO: Well, Horatio, you tremble
　　And look pale. Do you still think
　　It is just our imagination?

HORATIO: As God is my witness,
　　I wouldn't have believed this, but
　　I have seen it with my own eyes.

MARCELLUS: Isn't it like the king?

HORATIO: As you are like yourself!
That was the very armor he wore
When he fought the king of Norway.
I don't know what to think.
But it seems like a bad sign.

MARCELLUS: I think you are right.
But tell me this, if you can:
Why does our country seem to be
Preparing for a war?

HORATIO: I believe I know the reason.
Our last king, whose ghost we just saw,
Fought King Fortinbras of Norway.
The two kings had agreed that the winner
Would take the land of both countries.
When King Hamlet killed King Fortinbras,
Denmark took Norway's land.
Now the son of King Fortinbras,
Young Fortinbras, has put together
An army to take back the lands
Lost by his father. As I understand it,
This is the reason that we are
Preparing for war throughout our land.

BARNARDO: I think you are right, Horatio.
That is why this ghost comes to us
Dressed in armor and looking like the king
Who was and is the main issue of the war.

(*The* GHOST *enters again.*)

HORATIO: Ghost, if you can, speak to me!
If you want us to do something, say so!

If you know of something bad that may
Happen to Denmark, tell us.
Maybe we can avoid it if we know about it.
If something else is causing your spirit pain,
Speak of it. Stay and speak!

(*A rooster crows, and the* GHOST *exits.*)

MARCELLUS: It was about to speak
When the rooster crowed.

HORATIO: I have heard that spirits
Must leave the earth when it is day.
What we have seen proves that theory.
I think we should tell young Hamlet
What we have seen.

MARCELLUS: I agree. And I think I know
Where to find him. Let's go.

(MARCELLUS *and* HORATIO *exit.*)

# Scene 2

*The king's court.* KING CLAUDIUS, QUEEN GERTRUDE,
VOLTEMAND, CORNELIUS, POLONIUS, LAERTES, PRINCE
HAMLET, *and others enter.*

KING: The death of my brother Hamlet,
Is a memory still fresh in our minds.
It was good that the whole kingdom
Mourned for him. But common sense
Tells us that life goes on, and that
Our country needs a king and a queen.
That is why I have married my former
Sister-in-law, Queen Gertrude.
You all know, too, that Young Fortinbras

Thinks he can take advantage of our grief.
He has demanded that we give up
The land lost by his father to my brother.
That is the reason for this meeting.
I've written to the present king of Norway,
The uncle of Young Fortinbras.
Weak and bedridden, he hardly knows
Of his nephew's plans. I want you,
Cornelius and Voltemand, to take this
Letter to the old king of Norway.
(*He hands them a letter.*)
Farewell, and please hurry.

CORNELIUS and VOLTEMAND: Yes, my lord.

(*They bow and exit.*)

KING (*to* LAERTES): And now, Laertes,
You mentioned a request. What is it?

LAERTES: My lord, I ask your permission
To go back to France. I returned here
To show my loyalty at your coronation.
Now, my thoughts and wishes bend toward
France. I ask your gracious consent.

KING: Is it all right with your father?
What do you say, Polonius?

POLONIUS: He has received my consent.

KING: Enjoy yourself while you are young,
Laertes. Use your talents as you think best.
(LAERTES *bows. The* KING *turns to* HAMLET.)
Now, my nephew Hamlet, and my son—

HAMLET (*aside*): Your nephew, yes—
But hardly your *son.*

KING: You are still under a dark cloud.

HAMLET: Not so, my lord.
    I'm suffering from too much *sun*.

QUEEN: Hamlet, you must stop mourning.
    You know that death is natural.
    Everything that lives must die.

KING: It is fine to mourn for your father,
    But it is not healthy to cry for so long.
    Your father lost a father.
    And that father also lost his.
    I ask you to stop grieving and think of me
    As your father. You are heir to the throne.
    Your wish to return to Wittenberg to study
    Is the opposite of what we want.
    We want you to stay here in Denmark,
    As our chief courtier, kinsman, and son.

QUEEN: Please, Hamlet, stay here with us.

HAMLET: I shall obey you, Mother,
    To the best of my ability.

KING: That is a loving and fair answer.
    (*to the* QUEEN) Madam, come.

(*All exit but* HAMLET.)

HAMLET: Oh, if only this too too solid flesh
    Would melt, thaw, and turn itself into dew.
    Or if only suicide were not wrong.
    Oh, God! God! How weary, stale, and flat
    Everything in this world seems!
    He's not even been dead for two months,
    So excellent a king! He was so loving
    To my mother that he wouldn't even let

The winds blow too roughly on her face.
Why, she would hold on to him as if
She couldn't bear to let go!
Yet in less than two months—
Oh, God! Married to my father's brother,
But no more like my father
Than I am like Hercules!
Let me not think of it!
Frailty, your name is woman!
This marriage can come to no good.
Break, my heart. I must hold my tongue.

(HORATIO, MARCELLUS, *and* BARNARDO *enter.*)

HORATIO: Greetings to your lordship.

HAMLET: Hello, Horatio.
What brings you here from Wittenberg?

HORATIO: My lord, your father's funeral.

HAMLET: Please don't mock me, Horatio.
I think you came for my mother's wedding.

HORATIO: Indeed, it followed soon after.

HAMLET: It was thrifty, Horatio. The food
Left over from the funeral was served cold
For the wedding breakfast.
I wish I had never seen that day!
My father, I think I can see my father—

HORATIO (*surprised*): Where, my lord?

HAMLET: In my mind's eye, Horatio.

HORATIO: He was a fine king.

HAMLET: He was a man, all in all.
I shall not look upon his like again.

HORATIO: I think I saw him last night.

HAMLET: My father?

HORATIO: Yes, my lord.

HAMLET: Tell me more!

HORATIO: Marcellus and Barnardo saw him
Two nights in a row, while on watch.
They told me about it, and I kept watch
On the third night with them.
It happened again. I knew your father.
This ghost looked just like him.

HAMLET: But where was this?

MARCELLUS: My lord, outside the castle.

HAMLET: Did you speak to it?

HORATIO: I did, but it did not reply.

HAMLET: It is very strange.

HORATIO: But I swear it is true.
We thought it our duty to tell you.

HAMLET: Indeed, sirs, you were right.
Are you on watch tonight?

ALL: We are, my lord.

HAMLET: I will watch with you.
Maybe it will walk again.
If it looks like my father,
I will speak to it. I'll see you tonight.
(*All exit but* HAMLET.)
My father's spirit! All is not well.
I suspect foul play. I wish it were night.
Until then, my soul, sit tight.

# Scene 3

*Polonius's house.* LAERTES *and* OPHELIA *enter.*

LAERTES: My bags are already on board.
　　Farewell, my sister. Write often.

OPHELIA: Of course, dear brother.

LAERTES: As for Hamlet, and his actions—
　　Don't take his attentions to you seriously.
　　They are like violets in the spring.
　　Fast-blooming, sweet, but not long-lasting.

OPHELIA: No more than that?

LAERTES: No. He might love you now,
　　But remember who he is. As prince,
　　He may not choose a wife on his own.
　　His choice must be for the country's good.
　　If he says he loves you, be very careful.
　　Do not give your love too fast.
　　If you lose your honor or your heart,
　　You might also lose your good name.
　　Be very careful.

OPHELIA: I'll take your words to my heart.
　　But, my dear brother, I hope you follow
　　Your own advice, too.

LAERTES: Don't worry about me.
　　(POLONIUS, *their father, enters.*)
　　I have to go. But here comes our father.
　　I'll say good-bye to him again.

POLONIUS: Still here, Laertes?
　　Get aboard! Shame on you!
　　The wind is just right for sailing,

*10*

And they are waiting for you.
But listen first: I have some advice for you.
Be friendly, but don't be vulgar.
Be loyal to the friends you have
Who have proven themselves to be true.
But do not give the hand of friendship
Too easily to every new person you meet.
Listen much, but say little.
Dress as well as you can afford,
But do not be guided just by fashion.
Buy good—but not gaudy—clothing.
The clothing often says a lot about a man.
Neither a borrower nor a lender be, for
A loan often loses both the money
And the friend. And borrowing often makes
You spend more than you can afford.
This above all: to your own self be true.
And it must follow as night follows the day,
You cannot then be false to any man.
Farewell. May my blessings go with you!

LAERTES: Farewell, dear father.
Farewell, Ophelia. Remember what I said.

OPHELIA: It is locked in my memory,
And you yourself shall keep the key.

(LAERTES *exits*.)

POLONIUS: What did he say, Ophelia?

OPHELIA: Something about Prince Hamlet.

POLONIUS: Indeed. I'm glad he did.
I have heard lately that you and Hamlet
Have been spending time alone.

If so, I must tell you that you don't
Understand what people might say.
What's going on between you?
Tell me the truth.

OPHELIA: He has shown me lately
That he has affection for me.

POLONIUS: Affection? Bah!
Do you believe him?

OPHELIA: I do not know what to think.

POLONIUS: Well, then, I will teach you.
Be very careful, or you'll look like a fool.

OPHELIA: Father, he has courted me
In an honorable way.

POLONIUS: Really, now!
Don't mistake his passing interest for love.
From now on, don't be so available.
In fact, from this time on,
I don't want you to talk to Prince Hamlet.
These are my final words. Do as I say.

OPHELIA: I shall obey, Father.

(OPHELIA *and* POLONIUS *exit.*)

# Scene 4

*Outside the castle walls.* HAMLET, HORATIO, *and*
MARCELLUS *enter.*

HAMLET: It is so cold!

HORATIO: Yes, it is a chilly and bitter wind.

HAMLET: What time is it?

HORATIO: Not quite midnight.

MARCELLUS: No, it is just past midnight.

HORATIO: Indeed? Then it is almost time
For the ghost to take its walk.
(*The* GHOST *enters.*)
Look, my lord. It comes.

HAMLET: May the angels help us!
(*to the* GHOST) Do you come for good
Or for evil? You come in a form that is
Easy for me to talk to. I'll call you Hamlet,
King, father, and royal Dane. Answer me!
Don't keep me ignorant. Please tell me
Why your bones, blessed at your funeral,
Have left the grave. What does it mean,
That you, a corpse, walk at night
In the armor of battle? Why?
What do you want us to do?

(*The* GHOST *beckons to* HAMLET.)

HORATIO: It beckons you to go with it.
It must want to speak to you alone.

MARCELLUS: See how it waves you
Toward a place away from us.
Do not go with it.

HORATIO: No, by no means.

HAMLET: It will not speak here.
I must follow it.

HORATIO: Do not, my lord.

HAMLET: Why, what should I fear?
My life is not worth the price of a pin.
As for my soul, what could it do to that?
It waves me forth again. I'll follow it.

HORATIO: What if it leads you into danger?

HAMLET: It's still waving to me.
(*to the* GHOST) Go on. I'll follow you.

MARCELLUS (*holding him back*): Don't go!

HAMLET: Take your hands away!

HORATIO: Do as we say. Do not go!

HAMLET (*struggling*): My fate cries out.
Every vein in my body is as brave as a lion.
Let me go, gentlemen.
(*to the* GHOST) Go on. I'll follow you.

(*The* GHOST *and* HAMLET *exit.*)

HORATIO: He is going crazy!

MARCELLUS: Let's follow them.

HORATIO: What is this all about?

MARCELLUS: Something is rotten
In the state of Denmark.

HORATIO: Heaven will take care of it.

MARCELLUS: No! We must follow him.

(HORATIO *and* MARCELLUS *exit.*)

# Scene 5

*Outside the castle walls. The* GHOST *and* HAMLET *enter.*

GHOST: Listen carefully to what I say.

HAMLET: Speak, and I will hear you.

GHOST: I am your father's ghost.
I want you to revenge my foul and
Most unnatural murder.

HAMLET: Murder!

GHOST: Murder most foul, as it always is.
But this is the most horrible, strange,
And unnatural.

HAMLET: Tell me what you know, so
That I may sweep to my revenge!

GHOST: Hamlet, listen to me.
The story is told that I was sleeping
In my garden when a snake bit me.
That is not true. The snake that bit me
Is now wearing my crown!

HAMLET: Oh, just as I thought! My uncle!

GHOST: Yes, that beast!
First he stole my queen. Oh, Hamlet,
What a fall that was for her!
To go from me, whose love was true,
To that wretch who is so far below me!
But quickly: I can smell the morning air.
I will be brief. I was sleeping in my garden,
As was my custom, when your uncle
Poured poison into my ear.
As swift as quicksilver, it coursed through
My body. Thus, as I slept, I was killed
By my own brother's hand. In one moment,
I lost life, crown, and queen.
Oh horrible! Oh horrible! Most horrible!
If you have any feelings in you,
You must avenge me. But do nothing

Against your mother. Leave her to heaven.
Farewell now. Remember me!

(*The* GHOST *disappears.*)

HAMLET: Remember you? Yes, by heaven!
    Oh, that most evil woman! Oh, that villain!
    Remember you? I swear on it!

(HORATIO *and* MARCELLUS *enter.*)

HORATIO: My lord, my lord!

MARCELLUS: What happened?

HAMLET: There's a villain in Denmark
    Who is evil through and through.

HORATIO: We didn't need a ghost
    To tell us that.

HAMLET: You are absolutely right.
    But you must swear one thing.
    Never tell anyone what you saw tonight.

HORATIO and MARCELLUS: We swear.

HAMLET: Swear upon my sword.

HORATIO: We have already sworn.

GHOST (*from below*): Swear!

(HORATIO *and* MARCELLUS *swear on the sword of*
HAMLET.)

HORATIO: This is strange!

HAMLET: There are more things
    In heaven and earth, Horatio,

Than are dreamt of in your philosophy.
Here, as before, swear that you shall
Never speak a word about this.

GHOST: Swear!

(*They swear for the third time.*)

HAMLET (*to the* GHOST): Rest, rest,
  Troubled spirit.
  (*to* HORATIO *and* MARCELLUS)
  Many thanks for swearing on my sword!
  Don't forget now—not a word!

(HAMLET, HORATIO, *and* MARCELLUS *exit.*)

# Act 2

*Polonius sends a messenger to visit Laertes in Paris. Ophelia tells Polonius that Hamlet is acting very strange. Polonius decides that it is because Hamlet is sick with love for Ophelia. He reports Hamlet's strange behavior to the king and the queen. The king and the queen ask Rosencrantz and Guildenstern to spy on Hamlet.*

*Cornelius and Voltemand return from Norway with news that Young Fortinbras has agreed not to attack Denmark.*

*A traveling group of actors arrives to put on a play at the castle. Hamlet asks them to include a few new lines. He thinks these lines will cause a reaction in the king. This reaction will prove the king's guilt in his brother's death.*

## Scene 1

*Polonius's house.* POLONIUS *and* REYNALDO *enter.*

POLONIUS: Give him this money and
    These messages, Reynaldo.

REYNALDO: I will, my lord.

POLONIUS: I would also like you to
    Find out what other people are saying
    About Laertes. Say that you know him,
    But not very well. Then say something like,
    "I hear that he is very wild,
    Addicted to this and that, and so on."
    But say nothing that might dishonor him.
    Just mention the usual wild actions
    That are often associated with youth.

REYNALDO: Such as gambling, my lord?

POLONIUS: Yes, or drinking, fencing,
Swearing, quarreling, or wild women.
You could go that far.

REYNALDO: But that would dishonor him!

POLONIUS: Not really. Tone it down.
Make it sound as if you've heard that
He's a bit wild because of his lively mind.
If you suggest that he's been gambling,
People might then admit that they saw him.
I just want to know what he's really up to.
Do you understand?

REYNALDO: Yes, my lord, I do.

POLONIUS: Farewell now.
Keep an eye on him.

REYNALDO: I shall, my lord.

POLONIUS: But let him have his fun!

REYNALDO: Of course, my lord.

(REYNALDO *exits.* OPHELIA *enters.*)

POLONIUS: Well, now, Ophelia.
What's the matter?

OPHELIA: Oh, Father, I'm so frightened.

POLONIUS: About what, my dear?

OPHELIA: As I was sewing in my room,
Lord Hamlet came in, shirt unbuttoned.
He had no hat on. His socks were dirty
And falling down around his ankles.

He had a look on his face
That I can hardly describe.
He seemed out of his mind.

POLONIUS: Mad for your love?

OPHELIA: My lord, I do not know,
But it seemed that way.

POLONIUS: What did he say?

OPHELIA: He took me by the wrist
And held me hard. Then he looked deeply
Into my face as if to draw it later.
He looked at me like that for a long time.
At last, he sighed so deeply and sadly
That it seemed to shatter his entire body.
Finally, he let me go and left the room.
He turned his head over his shoulder,
Looking back at me as he left.
I don't know how he found the door,
For he certainly didn't use his eyes!

POLONIUS: Come with me to tell the king.
This kind of love is dangerous.
It sounds as if Hamlet might harm himself!
Have you said anything cruel to him lately?

OPHELIA: No, Father. But, as you ordered,
I returned his letters and
Spent no time with him.

POLONIUS: That is what drove him mad!
I am sorry that I misunderstood him.
I thought he was just toying with you.

I have a jealous nature!
Come, we must tell the king.
This sort of thing, if kept secret, could lead
To far more grief than any of us need.

(POLONIUS *and* OPHELIA *exit*.)

# Scene 2

*The king's court. The* KING *and the* QUEEN,
ROSENCRANTZ, GUILDENSTERN, *and* ATTENDANTS *enter*.

KING: Welcome, dear Rosencrantz and
   Guildenstern! We have missed you!
   Thanks for coming on such short notice.
   We are sure that you have heard about
   The changes in Hamlet. He is different,
   Both inside and out. We think the death of
   His father has caused this change.
   You have been friends with him since
   Childhood. Perhaps you can get him
   To enjoy life again. Maybe you can also
   Find out if something else is bothering him.
   We might be able to help him,
   If we knew what was wrong.

QUEEN: Good gentlemen, Hamlet has
   Talked about you a great deal.
   I am sure that you are his best friends.
   Please spend some time with us here.
   Your visit will be royally rewarded.

ROSENCRANTZ: No reward is necessary.

GUILDENSTERN: We are happy to help.

KING: Thanks, Rosencrantz and
    Gentle Guildenstern.

QUEEN: Thanks, Guildenstern and
    Gentle Rosencrantz. I beg you to
    Visit Hamlet right away.

(ROSENCRANTZ *and* GUILDENSTERN *exit.* POLONIUS *enters.*)

POLONIUS: My good lord, the ambassadors
    Have returned from Norway.

KING: You always have good news!

POLONIUS: Have I, my lord?
    I also think I know the reason
    For Hamlet's madness.

KING: Oh, tell me more about that!

POLONIUS: First, see the ambassadors.
    My news will be the dessert to follow
    That great feast.

(POLONIUS *exits.*)

KING (*to* QUEEN): Dear Gertrude, he says
    That he knows why your son
    Has been acting so strangely.

QUEEN: I thought the reasons were clear:
    His father's death and our quick marriage.

KING: Well, perhaps it's something else.
    (POLONIUS *enters, with* VOLTEMAND *and* CORNELIUS.)
    Welcome, my good friends.
    What news do you have from Norway?

VOLTEMAND: The king of Norway thought
   That his nephew was preparing to attack
   Poland. When he found out the truth—
   That Fortinbras planned to attack you—
   He was shocked and upset. He sent orders
   To his nephew to stop his preparations.
   In brief, Fortinbras obeys his uncle.
   Instead, he will take his soldiers to Poland.
   The king of Norway asks your permission
   For his nephew to march through Denmark
   On the way to Poland.
   (VOLTEMAND *gives the* KING *a document.*)
   He sends his request on this document.

KING: When we have more time,
   We shall read and think about this request.
   Meantime, thank you for your efforts.
   Get some rest. Tonight we'll feast together.
   Welcome back home.

(VOLTEMAND *and* CORNELIUS *exit.*)

POLONIUS: That was good news.
   And now, my news about Hamlet.
   It's true that he's mad.
   It's a pity, but it's true.
   My daughter Ophelia has given me this.
   Listen. (*He reads from a letter.*)
   "To the heavenly and my soul's idol,
   The most beautified Ophelia."
   What a stupid word—beautified!
   Here's more: "Doubt that the stars are fire.
   Doubt that the sun does move.

Doubt truth to be a liar.
But never doubt that I love.
Oh, dear Ophelia, I am no good at poetry.
But I love you so much. Believe me.
I am yours forever, most dear lady,
As long as I live, Hamlet."
My daughter has shown me this because
I asked her to.

KING: But how has she responded to it?

POLONIUS: Well, when I first found out that
Hamlet was interested in her,
I asked her to stop talking to him.
I also told her to receive no gifts from him.
She has obeyed me. I think this is why
Hamlet fell into a deep sadness.
He kept getting worse, until he went mad.

KING (*to* QUEEN): Do you think this is it?

QUEEN: It could be.

POLONIUS: Have I ever been wrong before?

KING: Not that I know.
How can we test your idea?

POLONIUS: You know that he sometimes
Walks for hours at a time in the lobby?

QUEEN: So he does, indeed.

POLONIUS: At such a time, I'll have Ophelia
Come into the lobby, too.
You and I will be behind the wall tapestry,
Watching their meeting.

If he hasn't gone mad from his love for her,
I'll quit my job and become a farmer!

KING: We will try it.

(HAMLET *enters, reading a book.*)

QUEEN: See how sadly he comes, reading.

POLONIUS: Go away, both of you, please.
I'll speak to him alone. Please leave.
(KING, QUEEN, *and* ATTENDANTS *exit.*)
How is my good Lord Hamlet?

HAMLET: Well, thank you. And you?

POLONIUS: Do you know me, my lord?

HAMLET: Yes, of course. You sell fish.

POLONIUS: Not I, my lord.

HAMLET: I wish you were so honest.

POLONIUS: Honest, my lord?

HAMLET: Yes, sir. To be honest
Is to be one man in ten thousand.

POLONIUS: That's very true, my lord.

HAMLET: Do you have a daughter?

POLONIUS: I have, my lord.

HAMLET: Don't let her walk in the sun.
She could get hurt if you let her outside.

POLONIUS (*aside*): What's going on?
He talks about my daughter.
Yet he didn't know me at first.
He thought I sold fish. He is far gone.
When I was young, I suffered for love, too.
I was almost as bad as this.

**26**

I'll speak to him again.
(*to* HAMLET) What do you read, my lord?

HAMLET: Words, words, words.

POLONIUS: What do they say?

HAMLET: Slanders, sir. It says here that
Old men have gray beards and wrinkles.
Also that they lack brains, have weak legs,
And that their eyes are runny.
All of this, sir, I strongly believe,
But I don't think it should be written down.

POLONIUS (*aside*): This may be madness,
Yet there is method in it. I'll leave him,
And find a way to have Ophelia meet him.
(*to* HAMLET) My lord, I will take my leave.

HAMLET: You cannot, sir, take from me
Anything that I would not part with
More willingly—except my life,
Except my life, except my life.

POLONIUS: Farewell, my lord.

HAMLET (*aside*): These boring old fools!

(ROSENCRANTZ *and* GUILDENSTERN *enter.*)

POLONIUS: You seek the Lord Hamlet?
There he is.

ROSENCRANTZ: Thank you, sir.

(POLONIUS *exits.*)

GUILDENSTERN: My honored lord.

ROSENCRANTZ: My most dear lord.

HAMLET: My excellent good friends.

What news do you have?

ROSENCRANTZ: None, my lord, except that
The world has grown honest.

HAMLET: Then doomsday must be near.
But your news isn't true. Let me ask this:
What bad luck has brought you to prison?

GUILDENSTERN: Prison, my lord?

HAMLET: Denmark is a prison.

ROSENCRANTZ: Then the world is one.

HAMLET: But Denmark is the worst part.

ROSENCRANTZ: I don't think so, my lord.

HAMLET: Well, then, we disagree.
Nothing is either good or bad
Unless you think it is.

ROSENCRANTZ: Your ambition makes it so.
Denmark is too narrow for your mind.

HAMLET: There's more to it than that.
But tell me, what brings you to Elsinore?

ROSENCRANTZ: To visit you, my lord.
No other reason.

HAMLET: Thank you. But tell me the truth.
Weren't you sent for? Come, come. Speak.

GUILDENSTERN: What should we say?

HAMLET: The truth. I can tell by the way
You look at me that the good king
And queen have sent for you.

ROSENCRANTZ: To do what, my lord?

HAMLET: That is what I want to know.
But let me ask you, as a friend,
To be honest with me.

ROSENCRANTZ (*aside to* GUILDENSTERN):
What are you going to say?

HAMLET: Now, I'm watching you.
If you are my friend, don't hold back.

GUILDENSTERN: My lord, we were sent for.

HAMLET: I will tell you why. That way,
You won't have to break your word to the
king and queen.
Lately, I don't know why,
I have lost all my joy.
Indeed, this whole earth seems to be
Nothing more than a dead rock.
Even the majestic sky seems like a foul
And poisonous collection of gases.
What a piece of work is Man!
How noble in reason! How infinite in mind!
How beautiful in form and motion!
How like an angel in action!
How like a god in understanding!
He is the most beautiful creature on earth!
And yet, to me, what is this piece of dust?
Man does not delight me—
No, nor Woman either,
Though your smiling face seems to imply it.

ROSENCRANTZ: My lord, I was thinking
No such thing.

HAMLET: Why did you laugh, then,

When I said that Man does not delight me?

ROSENCRANTZ: I was thinking that,
If you delight not in Man, the actors
Who are coming will get a dull welcome.
We passed them on the way here, and
They are on their way to entertain you.

HAMLET: Which actors are they?

ROSENCRANTZ: Ones you used to like—
The tragedy-actors from the city.

HAMLET: Why are they traveling?
They did very well in the theater.
It was good for their reputation and profit.

ROSENCRANTZ: I think they had troubles
In the city, but I'm not sure.

HAMLET: Are they as well liked as before?

ROSENCRANTZ: No, indeed, they are not.

HAMLET: Why? Have they grown rusty?

ROSENCRANTZ: No, they are still good.
But there is a group of child-actors
That now competes with them.
The child-actors are all the rage.

HAMLET: What, they are children?
Who manages them?
Who takes care of them? Will they quit
Acting when their voices change?

ROSENCRANTZ: I don't know, my lord?
But anyway, that is why these actors
Are on the road now.

*(Trumpets sound, announcing the* ACTORS.*)*

GUILDENSTERN: There they are.

HAMLET: My friends, I am glad you're here
    At Elsinore. But I must tell you,
    My uncle-father and aunt-mother
    Are wrong about me.

GUILDENSTERN: In what way, my lord?

HAMLET: I am mad only when
    The wind blows in a certain direction.
    When the wind comes from the south,
    I know what's what and who's who.

(POLONIUS *enters*.)

POLONIUS: Greetings to you, gentlemen.

HAMLET (*to* ROSENCRANTZ *and* GUILDENSTERN):
    Listen, you two. (*He points to* POLONIUS)
    That old infant you see there is not yet
    Out of his baby clothes.

ROSENCRANTZ: Maybe the old man
    Is in his second childhood.

HAMLET: I predict that he comes to tell me
    About the actors.

POLONIUS: My lord, I have news for you.
    The actors are here.

HAMLET (*winking at his friends*): Really!

POLONIUS: Upon my honor!

(*The* ACTORS *enter*.)

HAMLET: Welcome, gentlemen!

33

(*to* POLONIUS) My good lord,
Will you see that the actors
Have comfortable rooms?
Make sure that they are well cared for.
(*to* ACTORS) Follow him, friends.
We'll hear a play tomorrow.
(*to* FIRST ACTOR) Do you know the play,
"The Murder of Gonzago?"

FIRST ACTOR: Yes, my lord.

HAMLET: We'll have it tomorrow night.
Would you be able to learn a new speech
Of maybe 12 or 16 lines, which I'll write
And add at a certain point in the play?

FIRST ACTOR: Yes, my lord.

HAMLET: Good.
(*to all the* ACTORS) Follow that lord,
And see that you do not mock him.
(POLONIUS *and the* ACTORS *exit. To*
ROSENCRANTZ *and* GUILDENSTERN)
My good friends, I'll see you tonight.
I'm glad you're here at Elsinore.

ROSENCRANTZ: Good, my lord. Until then.

(ROSENCRANTZ *and* GUILDENSTERN *exit.*)

HAMLET: I have heard that guilty men,
While watching a play, have been made
To feel their guilt. I'll have these actors
Act out something like my father's murder

In front of my uncle. I'll watch him closely.
If he reacts, I'll know what to do.
I'd like to trust the words of the ghost,
But I also want my own proof.
The play's the thing
In which I'll catch the conscience of the king.

(HAMLET *exits.*)

# Act 3

*Rosencrantz and Guildenstern tell the king
and the queen that Hamlet seems to be fine.
The king and Polonius eavesdrop on the meet-
ing between Ophelia and Hamlet. Hamlet tells
Ophelia that he never loved her. Convinced that
Hamlet is dangerous, the king arranges for
Hamlet to go to England.*

*Hamlet gives the actors his additions to the
play. While watching the performance of this
scene, the king becomes upset.*

*Polonius hides in the queen's room while
Hamlet visits her. Mistaking him for the king,
Hamlet kills Polonius through the curtains.*

## Scene 1

*The castle lobby. The* KING, *the* QUEEN, POLONIUS,
OPHELIA, ROSENCRANTZ, *and* GUILDENSTERN *enter.*

KING (*to* ROSENCRANTZ *and* GUILDENSTERN):
    He didn't tell you why
    He's been acting so strange?

ROSENCRANTZ: Not at all. He admits that
    He doesn't feel like himself.
    But he didn't tell us why.

QUEEN: Did he receive you well?

GUILDENSTERN: Like a true gentleman.

QUEEN: Was he interested in any pastime?

ROSENCRANTZ: Madam, it so happened
    That we met some actors on our way here.

We told him about it, and he seemed glad.
They are here now, and Hamlet has already
Asked them to put on a play this evening.

POLONIUS: That's true. He would like it if
Your majesties attend the play tonight.

KING: With all my heart, I am happy
To hear that he's interested in something.
Good gentlemen, tell him we'll be there.

ROSENCRANTZ: We shall, my lord.

(ROSENCRANTZ *and* GUILDENSTERN *exit.*)

KING: Gertrude, please leave us, too.
We have sent for Hamlet so that he may,
As if by accident, meet Ophelia.
Her father and I will hide nearby.
We want to see if he is suffering from love.

QUEEN: I shall obey you.
As for you, Ophelia, I do wish that
Love of you is the happy cause
Of Hamlet's madness. I hope that
Your goodness will bring him back to
Normal again, for the good of both of you.

OPHELIA: Madam, I hope so, too.

(*The* QUEEN *exits.*)

POLONIUS (*to* OPHELIA): Walk here, dear,
And read this book of prayers.
That way, it won't appear strange that
You are alone.
(*to the* KING) My lord, we will hide here.
I hear him! Quick. Hide.

(*The* KING *and* POLONIUS *exit.* HAMLET *enters.*)

HAMLET (*to himself*): To be or not to be,
     That is the question. Is it nobler in the mind
     To suffer the slings and arrows
     Of outrageous fortune? Or is it better
     To take arms against a sea of trouble,
     And by fighting, end them?
     To die is to sleep—no more than that.
     By this sleep, we can end the heartaches
     And the thousand natural shocks
     That our bodies must suffer. It is an ending
     To be warmly welcomed. To die, to sleep;
     To sleep, perhaps to dream—
     Ay, there's the rub. In that sleep of death,
     What dreams may come?
     When we have cast off this mortal body,
     Who knows what dreams might appear?
     We suffer the pains of life for so long
     Because we dread the trip
     To that unknown country, from which
     No traveler ever returns.
     Who wants to leave the pains of this life
     And fly to others that we know not of?
     So conscience makes cowards of us all.
     (*He sees* OPHELIA.) Young lady,
     In your prayers, remember my sins.

OPHELIA: My lord, how are you lately?

HAMLET: I humbly thank you. I am well.

OPHELIA: I have some gifts of yours
     That I've wanted to return for some time.
     I'd appreciate it if you'd take them now.

**38**

HAMLET: No, not I.
    I never gave you anything.

OPHELIA: My lord, you know you did.
    And you said such sweet words,
    Words that added richness to the gifts.
    But since their perfume has faded,
    Take them back again. To sensitive people,
    Fine gifts mean nothing when the givers
    No longer care.

HAMLET: I did love you once.

OPHELIA: Indeed, my lord.
    You made me believe that you did.

HAMLET: You shouldn't have believed me.
　　Actually, I never really loved you.

OPHELIA: You had me fooled.

HAMLET: Go to a nunnery. That is better
　　Than becoming a mother to sinners!
　　Why should such creatures as ourselves
　　Be crawling between earth and heaven?
　　All men are scoundrels. Believe none of us.
　　You'd be better off in a convent.
　　Where's your father?

OPHELIA: At home, my lord.

HAMLET: Lock him in. That way,
　　He can act the fool only at home.
　　As for you, if you must marry,
　　Marry a fool. Wise men know too well
　　How wicked you might be.
　　I say we will have no more marriages.
　　Those who are married already, all but one,
　　Can stay married. The rest shall not marry.
　　To a nunnery, go.

(HAMLET *exits.*)

OPHELIA: Oh, help him, you sweet heavens!
　　What a noble mind has lost its reason!
　　And I, the most wretched of women.
　　I heard the music of his loving promises,
　　Now the music is harsh and out of tune.
　　Oh, woe is me,
　　To have seen what I have seen, see what
　　　　I see.

(*The* KING *and* POLONIUS *enter.*)

KING: Love? I don't think so!
 I don't think he is mad, either.
 There's something in his soul
 That is making him very unhappy.
 It also might be dangerous. To avoid it,
 I have decided to send him to England.
 The king there owes us some money, and
 Hamlet can collect it. What do you think?

POLONIUS: That is a good idea.
 But I still think that his unhappiness is
 Caused by unfulfilled love for my daughter.
 (*to* OPHELIA) All right, Ophelia!
 You don't have to tell us what he said.
 We heard it all. (*to the* KING) My lord,
 Do as you please. But may I suggest this:
 After the play, let his mother meet with him
 In private. Perhaps she can get him to talk.
 I'll hide in her room so I can hear them.
 If he does not tell her the real reasons
 For his grief, then send him to England.
 Or, you could lock him up in a place
 Where, in your wisdom, you think best.

KING: It shall be so.
 Madness in great ones must not unwatched go.

(*All exit.*)

# Scene 2

*Inside the castle.* HAMLET *and three* ACTORS *enter.*

HAMLET: Say the speech, as I told you to.
 Pronounce it trippingly on the tongue.
 Do not overact the part. Just be natural.

Do not make too many dramatic gestures.
Oh, it offends me to the soul when an actor
Tears a passion to tatters, to very rags.
Such an actor should be whipped!
I ask you to avoid such acting.

FIRST ACTOR: Of course, my lord.

HAMLET: But don't be too dull, either.
Use your own judgment.
Suit the action to the word,
The word to the action.
Remember that the purpose of acting is
To hold a mirror up to nature.
Show things as they are, in other words.

FIRST ACTOR: I think we can do that, sir.

HAMLET: I hope so. Go and get ready.
(ACTORS *exit*. POLONIUS *enters*.)
Well, now, my lord,
Will the king be attending the play tonight?

POLONIUS: Yes, and the queen will, too.

HAMLET: Tell the actors to hurry.
(POLONIUS *exits*. HORATIO *enters*.)
Hello, Horatio!

HORATIO: My lord, I am at your service.

HAMLET: Horatio, my friend, you are
The most sensible man I have ever known.

HORATIO: Oh, my dear lord!

HAMLET: I'm not saying this to flatter you.
What advantage would I hope to gain
From a man whose only wealth

Is in his own good spirits?
Why should anyone flatter the poor?
Ever since I could tell the difference
Between the qualities of different men,
I have chosen you as a friend.
Even though you have had some bad luck,
You have never complained about it.
You always take the bad with the good.
Blessed are those who can keep on going,
No matter what fate has in store. Give me
That man who is not passion's slave.
I will take him to my heart, as I do you.
But enough of this.
There is a play tonight before the king.
One scene is very close to the circumstance
Which I have told you of my father's death.
When that act is being performed,
Please watch my uncle very carefully.
If his hidden guilt does not show up then,
I'll be very surprised. While you watch him,
I will be watching him, too.
Later, we can compare our judgments
About his behavior.

HORATIO: Yes indeed, my lord.

HAMLET: I hear them coming now.
I'll have to start my mad act again.
Find yourself a seat.

(KING, QUEEN, POLONIUS, OPHELIA, ROSENCRANTZ,
GUILDENSTERN, *and* ATTENDANTS *enter.*)

KING: How are you tonight, Hamlet?

HAMLET: Excellent! I've been eating
    The same food as chameleons do:
    Fresh air and empty promises. You cannot
    Feed chickens that way.

KING: What are you saying, Hamlet?
    These words mean nothing to me.

HAMLET: No, nor to me.
    (*to* POLONIUS) My lord, you acted once,
    In a play at the university, didn't you?

POLONIUS: That I did, my lord.
    I was a fairly good actor.

HAMLET: What part did you play?

POLONIUS: I was Julius Caesar.
    I was murdered in the Capitol.
    Brutus killed me.

HAMLET: What a brute he was to kill
    So capital an idiot there!
    Are the actors ready?

ROSENCRANTZ: Yes, my lord.

QUEEN: Come here, my dear Hamlet.
    Sit by me.

HAMLET: No, good mother.
    I'm drawn to something more attractive.

(HAMLET *turns toward* OPHELIA.)

POLONIUS (*aside to the* KING): Oh, ho!
    Did you hear that?

HAMLET (*lying down at* OPHELIA'S *feet*):
    Lady, shall I lie in your lap?

OPHELIA (*blushing*): No, my lord.

HAMLET: I mean, my head upon your lap.

OPHELIA: Well, yes. That would be fine.
  You are in a better mood than before.

HAMLET: Why shouldn't I be? After all,
  Look at how cheerful my mother is,
  And my father dead less than two hours.

OPHELIA: It's been four months, my lord.

HAMLET: So long? My word.
  Dead four months and not yet forgotten!
  So there's some hope that a great man
  Might even be remembered for six months!

(*Trumpets sound. A show in pantomime follows.
It opens as a king and a queen enter. They
embrace each other. Then he lies down on a bed
of flowers. Seeing him asleep, she leaves him.
Soon, a villain enters. He removes the king's
crown and kisses it. Then he pours poison in the
sleeping king's ears, and leaves him. The queen
returns, finds the king dead, and cries. The villain enters again, with three or four others. They
seem to share the queen's grief. The dead body
is carried away. The villain woos the queen with
gifts. She seems cool at first, but in the end
accepts his love. Everyone exits.*)

OPHELIA: What does this mean, my lord?

HAMLET: It means mischief.

OPHELIA: Perhaps this mime show is
  A hint about the play we will be seeing.

HAMLET: We shall soon see.

(*The* ACTOR KING *and* ACTOR QUEEN *enter.*)

ACTOR KING: It has been 30 years
    Since we two fell in love and got married.

ACTOR QUEEN: And may we be happy for
    Another 30 years. But woe is me!
    You have been so ill lately.
    I am worried about you.

ACTOR KING: Yes, I am sorry.
    It looks as if I will be leaving you soon.
    I am not as strong as I used to be.
    My honored and beloved wife, perhaps
    You'll meet another—

ACTOR QUEEN: —Oh, don't say that!
    There will never be another one for me!
    If I married again, I would be cursed.
    None marry a second
    Except those who killed the first.

HAMLET (*aside*): What a bitter thought!

ACTOR QUEEN: The only reason to marry
    A second time is for money.
    Certainly not for love!

ACTOR KING: I'm sure you mean that now.
    But later, you might break that vow.
    Nothing is forever, so it's not strange
    That even our loves will change.
    For here's a question we have yet to prove:
    Does love decide our fate, or fate our love?

You say you will no second husband wed.
That might change when the first is dead.

ACTOR QUEEN: Dear, I swear this is true,
The only husband I'll ever have is you!

ACTOR KING: What a solemn vow!
Sweet, please leave. Let me sleep now.

ACTOR QUEEN: May sleep come to you.
And may nothing ever divide us two.

(ACTOR QUEEN *exits*. ACTOR KING *sleeps*.)

HAMLET: Mother, how do you like
This play so far?

QUEEN: I think the lady protests too much.

HAMLET: Perhaps, but they are just acting.
The poison isn't real.

KING: What is the title of the play?

HAMLET: The Mousetrap. It is based on a
Real-life story of a murder in Vienna.
Gonzago is the Duke's name.
His wife's name is Baptista. You'll see.
But what does it matter your majesty?
For those of us with clear consciences—
The play has nothing to do with us.
(ACTOR VILLAIN *enters*.) Watch this!
This is the good part!

ACTOR VILLAIN: Evil thoughts, busy hands,
Strong poison, and no one watching!
Perfect! This should take effect soon.

(ACTOR VILLAIN *pours poison into the ear of*
ACTOR KING.)

HAMLET: He poisons Gonzago
   In the garden, for his money.
   You shall soon see how the murderer wins
   The love of Gonzago's wife.

(KING CLAUDIUS *stands up.*)

OPHELIA: The king has risen to his feet.

HAMLET: Why? Did something scare him?

QUEEN (*to* KING): What is wrong, my lord?

POLONIUS: Stop the play.

KING: Turn on the lights. Let's go!

POLONIUS: Lights, lights, lights.

(*All exit but* HAMLET *and* HORATIO.)

HAMLET: Were you watching him?

HORATIO: Very closely, my lord.

HAMLET: And what did you think?

HORATIO: I think your suspicions are right.

(POLONIUS *enters.*)

POLONIUS: My lord, the queen would like
   To speak with you, right away.
   She is waiting in her room.

HAMLET: I will be there soon.

POLONIUS: I'll tell her, my lord.

(POLONIUS *exits.*)

HAMLET (*to* HORATIO *and the* ACTORS):
   Please leave me, my friends.

(HORATIO *and the* ACTORS *leave.*)
Now, I shall go see my mother.
Oh heart, do not lose your natural feelings!
Let me be cruel to her, but not unnatural.
I will speak daggers to her, but use none.
After all, she is my mother and I am her
son.

(HAMLET *exits.*)

# Scene 3

*Inside the castle.* KING, ROSENCRANTZ, *and*
GUILDENSTERN *enter.*

KING: I don't like the way he looks at me.
While he's mad, I don't feel safe.
So prepare to go to England with him.

GUILDENSTERN: Yes, your majesty.
It is our sacred duty to keep you safe.

ROSENCRANTZ: Many people rely on you.
The death of a king is bad for everyone.
We will do whatever we can for you.

(ROSENCRANTZ *and* GUILDENSTERN *exit.* POLONIUS
*enters.*)

POLONIUS: He's going to see his mother.
I'll hide behind her curtains so I can hear.
I'm sure she'll find out what's going on.
I'll call on you before you go to bed,
And tell you what I know.

KING: Thanks, my dear lord.
(POLONIUS *exits.*)
Oh, my crime is terrible!

It smells to heaven!
Like Cain in the Bible story,
I have murdered my own brother.
I can hardly pray, even though I want to.
My guilt prevents me from doing so.
What would I say in a prayer?
"Forgive me my terrible murder"?
I cannot be forgiven, for I still have
All the benefits I got from that murder.
My crown, my ambition, and my queen.
Can I be pardoned and still keep these?
In this world, money can buy out the law.
But this is not true in heaven.
What a wretched state!
Oh, my heart is as heavy and dark as death!
Help, angels! Do what you can.
Bow, stubborn knees. And, heart,
With strings of steel
Be soft as a new-born babe!
All may be well.

(*The* KING *kneels to pray.* HAMLET *enters.*)

HAMLET: Now I could do it easily.
    (*He draws his sword.*) But no!
    If I do it now, he would go to heaven.
    That would not be fair.
    A villain kills my father, and for that,
    I, his only son, send the villain to heaven.
    There is no revenge in that.
    He took my father by surprise.
    My father had no time to confess his sins.
    No! I shall wait. I will kill him later,

When he is doing something evil!
Then his soul will be kept out of heaven.

(HAMLET *exits*.)

KING (*rising to his feet*): My words fly up,
But my thoughts stay here below.
Empty words never to heaven go.

(*The* KING *exits*.)

# Scene 4

*The queen's chambers.* QUEEN *and* POLONIUS *enter*.

POLONIUS: He'll be here soon.
Now, be firm with him. Let him know
That his behavior has not been right.
I'll hide here silently.

(POLONIUS *hides behind the curtains*. HAMLET *enters*.)

HAMLET: Hello, Mother. What's wrong?

QUEEN: You have offended your father,
The mighty King Claudius.

HAMLET: No, you have offended my father,
The good King Hamlet.

QUEEN: Come, come.
What a foolish answer!

HAMLET: Go, go. What a wicked question!

QUEEN: Have you forgotten who I am?

HAMLET: No, I haven't. But you have.
Sit down, and don't move.
I will show you yourself in a mirror.

QUEEN: What are you going to do?
　　You don't plan to murder me? Help!

POLONIUS (*from behind curtains*): Help!

HAMLET: Who's that? A rat!

(*He thrusts his sword through the curtains.*)

POLONIUS: Oh, he has killed me!

QUEEN: Oh, my, what have you done?

HAMLET: I don't know. Is it the king?

(*He lifts the curtain and finds Polonius dead.*)

QUEEN: Oh, what a rash and bloody deed!

HAMLET: A bloody deed.
　　Almost as bad, good mother,
　　As killing a king and marrying his brother.

QUEEN: As killing a king, did you say?

HAMLET: Yes, lady, that's what I said.
　　Stop wringing your hands. Quiet.
　　Sit down, and let me wring your heart.

QUEEN: What have I done, that you dare
　　To speak to me in such a rude manner?

HAMLET: An act that makes marriage vows
　　As false as gamblers' promises.
　　Remember the man who was your husband.
　　So good he was almost like a god.
　　Compare him to your present husband.
　　Do you see the difference? Are you blind?

QUEEN: Oh, Hamlet, speak no more!
　　You've turned my eyes into my very soul.

There I see such evil spots,
That will never be clean.

HAMLET: A murderer and a villain.
A wretch that isn't worth the small toe
Of your former husband. A monster
Who stole the precious crown and
Put it in his pocket—

QUEEN: No more.

HAMLET: A king of rags and patches—
(GHOST *enters.*) Save me, protect me

With your wings, heavenly angels!
(*to* GHOST) What does your majesty wish?

QUEEN (*not seeing* GHOST): You're mad!

HAMLET: Have you come to scold your son
For not having taken revenge yet? Tell me.

GHOST: Your mother is suffering.
Step between her and her struggling soul.
Help her, Hamlet. (GHOST *exits.*)

HAMLET: Mother, I am sorry if I upset you.
I am not mad, either. You will find peace
Only in one way. You must confess
What you have done. Do not make it worse
By living as a wife to that villain, the king.

QUEEN: Son, you have cut my heart in two!

HAMLET: Then throw away the worse half,
And live more purely with the other half.
Good night. Do not go to my uncle's bed.
Pretend to be good even if you are not.
Stay away once. Next time will be easier;
And easier still after that. So, good night.
I must be cruel only to be kind.
One more thing, good lady.

QUEEN: What is it?

HAMLET: I have heard that I must go to England.
The king wishes it.
My two friends—whom I trust
As I trust snakes—will go with me.
They carry a letter from the king.

So be it: It's fun to see the hangman hanged
With his own noose. I know the plan,
And no one will get the better of me.
Now, I'll drag this body to the next room.
This body so still, so secret, and so grave.
Mother, at last good night.
I'll see you in the morning light.

(HAMLET *exits, dragging* POLONIUS *offstage. The*
QUEEN *remains*.)

# Act 4

The king finds out that Hamlet has killed Polonius, and realizes that he was the intended victim. He writes a letter to the king of England, asking that Hamlet be put to death when he arrives there. Hamlet leaves for England but returns to Denmark after a series of incidents.

The king and Laertes plan a duel, in which Laertes will use a poison-tipped sword against Hamlet. They also plan to have a poisoned drink for Hamlet, in case Laertes fails to stab him. Ophelia, having gone mad, drowns in a stream.

## Scene 1

*Inside the castle. The* KING *enters, joining the* QUEEN.

KING: These sighs must mean something.

QUEEN: Oh, the things I've seen tonight!

KING: What, Gertrude? How is Hamlet?

QUEEN: Mad as the wind in a storm.
   He heard a noise from behind the curtains,
   Cried out, "A rat," and killed Polonius.

KING: Oh, terrible deed!
   It would have been my fate if I'd been there!
   How will we explain this bloody deed?
   The people will blame me. I should have
   Had this mad young man locked up,
   But I loved him too much. Where is he?

QUEEN: He has taken the body away.

KING: Oh, Gertrude, we have to find him.
　　We'll send him away by ship this evening.
　　This evil deed must somehow be explained.

(ROSENCRANTZ *and* GUILDENSTERN *enter.*)

ROSENCRANTZ: You sent for us, my lord?

KING: Yes. Our plans have changed a little.
　　In his madness, Hamlet has killed Polonius.
　　He has dragged the body out of here.
　　Go find him, ask him where the body is,
　　And bring it to the chapel. Hurry, please.
　　(ROSENCRANTZ *and* GUILDENSTERN *exit.*)
　　Gertrude, we must see our wisest friends.
　　We shall tell them what has happened
　　And what we plan to do. Perhaps then they
　　Won't think we had anything to do with it.
　　Let's go. My soul is full of fear and dismay.

(*The* KING *and the* QUEEN *exit.*)

# Scene 2

*The castle lobby.* HAMLET *enters.*

HAMLET: There! The body is safely hidden!
　　(*Voices are heard, calling his name.*)
　　What is that? Who's calling me?

(ROSENCRANTZ *and* GUILDENSTERN *enter.*)

ROSENCRANTZ: Sir, where is the body?

HAMLET: I've mixed it with dust.

ROSENCRANTZ: Tell us where it is.

The king wants it brought to the chapel.

HAMLET: Why should I be questioned
By a sponge such as you?

ROSENCRANTZ: You take me for a sponge?

HAMLET: Yes, sir. You soak up the king's
Favors, rewards, and influence. When he
Needs to know what you have found out,
All he has to do is squeeze you. Then,
Like a sponge, you are dry again.

ROSENCRANTZ: I don't understand you, sir.

HAMLET: I'm not surprised. A good speech
Means nothing to a foolish ear.
Take me to the king.

(*All exit.*)

# Scene 3

*The king's court. The* KING *and several* LORDS *enter.*

KING: I have sent them to find Hamlet
And to find the body. Hamlet is dangerous!
Yet we must not lock him up.
He is too popular. To keep the peace,
His sudden leaving must seem planned.
(HAMLET *enters.*)
Now, Hamlet, where's Polonius?

HAMLET: At supper.

KING: At supper? Where?

HAMLET: Not where he eats,
But where the worms are eating him.

KING: Now, now. Tell us where he is.

HAMLET: In heaven. Send for him there.
     If you don't find him within a month,
     You'll smell him as you go up the stairs
     Into the lobby.

KING (*to some* LORDS): Go seek him there.

HAMLET: He will stay there till you come.

(LORDS *exit.*)

KING: Hamlet, for your own safety,
     We must send you with fiery quickness
     To England. So get ready. The ship waits,
     The wind is blowing, and everything is set.

HAMLET: So, I've heard. Fine! I'll get ready.

(HAMLET *exits.*)

KING (*to some* LORDS): Follow him closely.
     Make sure he gets on board right away.
     He must leave tonight. Hurry.
     (*All exit but the* KING.)
     King of England, if you value my goodwill,
     You'll do what I've asked in my letter.
     I want the immediate death of Hamlet.
     He rages like a sickness in my blood,
     And you must cure me. Until it is done,
     My joys in life will not have begun.

(*The* KING *exits.*)

# Scene 4

*The ship.* FORTINBRAS *enters, with a* CAPTAIN *and some soldiers.*

FORTINBRAS (*to* CAPTAIN): Please ask
     The Danish king if it is still all right

For us to march through his country
On our way to Poland.

CAPTAIN: Yes, my lord.

(*All but the* CAPTAIN *exit. Then* HAMLET,
ROSENCRANTZ, *and* GUILDENSTERN *enter.*)

HAMLET: Sir, whose army is that,
Who commands it, and why are they here?

CAPTAIN: Sir, it's the army of Norway,
Commanded by Fortinbras. We're going to
Poland to fight for a little patch of ground
That is not worth much.

HAMLET: Well, surely, the Polish king
Will not bother to defend it.

CAPTAIN: On the contrary, sir.
The Polish army is already there.

HAMLET: What a waste! Thousands of men
Will die defending a piece of earth that is
Worth nothing! Thank you, sir.

CAPTAIN: God be with you, sir. (*He exits.*)

ROSENCRANTZ: Ready to go, my lord?

HAMLET: In a moment. Go on ahead.
(*All exit but* HAMLET.)
How everything spurs me on to revenge!
What is a man, if his main activities are just
Sleeping and eating? No more than a beast.
Surely human beings are meant for more!
Sometimes I fail to act because I think
Too much about the consequences.
Look at young Fortinbras. Though he risks

Everything for an eggshell, at least
He acts to avenge his father!
To be great does not necessarily mean
To fight for noble causes. It might mean
To fight for a straw when honor is at stake.
What about me, then? My father is killed,
And my mother's honor is destroyed.
To my shame, I see 20,000 men go to war
Over land not big enough for their graves.
Oh, from this day until the end,
May all my actions be for revenge!

(HAMLET *exits*.)

# Scene 5

*Inside the castle. The* QUEEN, HORATIO, *and a*
GENTLEMAN *enter.*

QUEEN: What does Ophelia want?

GENTLEMAN: She speaks about her father.
Her words do not make much sense.

QUEEN: Send her in.

(GENTLEMAN *exits.* OPHELIA *enters*.)

OPHELIA: Where is the beautiful queen?

QUEEN: How are you, Ophelia?

OPHELIA (*singing*): "He is dead and gone,
Under the grass, at his head a stone."

QUEEN: But Ophelia—

OPHELIA: Listen to this (*she sings*):
"His shroud is as white as mountain snow.
He lies among sweet white flowers,

**61**

Watered with our tearful showers."

(*The* KING *enters.*)

QUEEN: Alas, look at her, my lord!

KING: She's obsessed with her father.

OPHELIA (*singing*): "Tomorrow is
Saint Valentine's Day.
Early in the morning time,
I'll be a maid at your window,
I'll be your valentine.
Then up he rose, put on his clothes,

And opened his bedroom door.
The maid came in and stayed awhile,
And was a maiden nevermore.
She said, 'Before you invited me in,
You promised we would wed!'
He said, 'It's true, I would have done it,
If you'd not come so quickly to my bed!'"

KING: How long has she been like this?

OPHELIA: I hope all will be well.
We must be patient. But I can't help crying
When I think of him lying
In the cold, cold ground. My brother shall
Hear of it. Thank you for everything.
Good night, ladies, good night.
Sweet ladies, good night, good night.

(OPHELIA *exits*.)

KING (*to* HORATIO): Follow her.
Watch her closely, will you?
(HORATIO *exits*.) This poison of her grief
Springs from her father's death.
Oh, Gertrude, Gertrude.
When sorrows come, they do not come
In single drops, but in floods.
First, her father was killed. Then,
Your son left. The people are confused.
They think I had something to do with
Polonius's death. And poor Ophelia,
No longer in control of her own mind.
Laertes has come back from France and
Has heard rumors about his father's death.
(*He hears a noise outside*.) What's that?

(*A* MESSENGER *enters.*) What's happening?

MESSENGER: Brace yourself, my lord.
    Young Laertes and his rebel force
    Have swept aside your own soldiers.
    The mob calls him "Lord" and says,
    "Laertes shall be king!"

KING: The doors are broken down!

(LAERTES *and some* FOLLOWERS *enter.*)

LAERTES : Where is the king?
    (*to his* FOLLOWERS) Sirs, stand outside.
    Guard the door. (FOLLOWERS *exit.*)
    (*to the* KING) Oh, you vile king!
    Give me back my father.

QUEEN: Calm down, good Laertes!

LAERTES: If one drop of my blood
    Stays calm, it would betray my father.

KING: Why are you so angry, Laertes?

LAERTES: My father is dead! How did this
    Come to happen? I want the truth!
    Come what may, I'll have revenge!

KING: Laertes, in avenging your father,
    Will you kill both friends and foes?

LAERTES: Only his enemies.

KING: Do you want to know who they are?

LAERTES: Of course.

KING: I am innocent of your father's death.
    I am deeply grieved by it. (OPHELIA *is heard
    singing.*) Let her come in.

LAERTES: Oh, heat, dry up my brains!

May salty tears burn out my eyes!
By heavens, your madness will be avenged!
Dear maid, kind sister, sweet Ophelia!
Is it possible that a young maid's mind
Is as fragile as an old man's life?

OPHELIA (*singing*): "There, at his grave,
Our tears we gave—"

LAERTES: If you were sane, you could not
Argue better for revenge.

KING: Laertes, I share your grief.
Go now and find your wisest friends.
They shall listen to both of us and judge.
If they find me guilty, then you shall have
My kingdom, my crown, my life,
And all else that I own. If not, be patient.
I will find a way to make up for your loss.

LAERTES: Let this be so.
The way he died, his secret funeral,
With no ceremonies to mark his passing—
All these things cry out for explanation.

KING: And have it you shall.
Where the guilt lies, let the great ax fall.

(*All exit.*)

# Scene 6

*Inside the castle walls.* HORATIO *and a* SERVANT *enter.*

HORATIO: Who wants to speak with me?

SERVANT: Seafaring men, sir. They say that
They have letters for you.

HORATIO: Send them in.

(SERVANT *exits.* SAILORS *enter.*)

FIRST SAILOR: Greetings to you, sir.

HORATIO: And to you.

FIRST SAILOR: I have a letter for you.
It's from the ambassador to England.

(*He hands the letter to* HORATIO.)

HORATIO (*reading*): "Dear Horatio,
When you've finished reading this,
Arrange for these fellows to meet the king.
They have letters for him. Pirates boarded
Our ship on our second day at sea.
In the ensuing battle, I boarded their ship.
When our ship got free, I found that I was
Their only prisoner. I've been treated well.
They expect a favor from me in return.
After the king gets the letters, join me
As fast as you would run away from death.
These fellows will take you to where I am.
Rosencrantz and Guildenstern are on their
Way to England. I have much to tell you.
Yours, Hamlet."
(*to* SAILORS) Come with me to the king.
Then you can take me to Hamlet.

(*All exit.*)

# Scene 7

*The king's court. The* KING *and* LAERTES *enter.*

KING: Now you know the truth.

You must realize that I am your friend.
After Hamlet killed your father,
He also tried to kill me.

LAERTES: It seems so. But tell me
Why you did not punish him.

KING: There were two reasons.
First, his mother lives almost for his looks.
And I love her too much to hurt her.
Second, the common people love him, too.
No matter what I would have said of him,
They would not have believed it.

LAERTES: So I have lost my noble father,
And my sister has gone mad.
My revenge will come.

KING: Do not lose any sleep over it.
Don't think that I am ready to forget
What Hamlet did. I loved your father,
And I love myself. I will have revenge
For what Hamlet did and tried to do.

(*A* MESSENGER *enters, with the letters.*)

MESSENGER: This is for your majesty.
And this one is for the queen.

KING: From Hamlet! Who brought them?

MESSENGER: Sailors, my lord.

(MESSENGER *exits.*)

KING: Laertes, you shall hear this.
(*reading:*) "Your majesty, I am back
In Denmark, stripped of all my belongings.
Tomorrow, I would like to meet with you

And tell you why I returned so suddenly."
What is the meaning of this?

LAERTES: Is it in his handwriting?

KING: Yes, it is.

LAERTES: Let him come. I did not dream
I could have my revenge so soon.

KING: I have a plan to make your revenge
Look like an accident.
Even his mother will think so.

LAERTES: What plan is that, my lord?

KING: I know you are good with a sword.
Hamlet thinks he is good, too. He is jealous
Of your reputation. He'd like nothing more
Than to fence with you in a public match.
Hamlet will soon know you've come home.
I'll arrange for people to praise your skill.
Soon there will be a contest between you.
Bets will be made on each of you.
He, trusting and unsuspecting,
Would never think to inspect the swords.
We'll have one tipped with poison.
You shall use it. Then, in one practice pass,
You can settle with him for your father.

LAERTES: I'll do it. I even have the poison.
It is so strong that there's no antidote.
I'll touch my point with this poison.
If I just scratch him with it, he will die.

KING: We should allow no room for error.
It would be better not to try than to fail.
For if we're found out, we will look bad.

Here's a backup plan: If you have trouble
With the sword, try to make him tired.
When he calls for something to drink,
I'll have a goblet prepared for him.
Of course, the drink will be poisoned.
If he happens to avoid the poisoned sword,
We'll get him with the goblet.

(*The* QUEEN *enters, in great distress.*)

QUEEN: One sorrow after another.
    Your sister is drowned, Laertes!

LAERTES: Drowned? Where?

QUEEN: She was making flower chains
    By the stream. Climbing to hang them
    From an overhanging tree branch, she fell
    Into the water when the branch broke off.
    Her clothes spread out, holding her up
    For a while. Then, heavy with water, they
    Pulled the poor wretch to muddy death.

LAERTES: Alas, then, she is drowned?

QUEEN: Drowned, drowned.

LAERTES: You've had too much water,
    Poor Ophelia, so I'll hold back my tears.
    But I'm only human. I cannot. (*He weeps.*)
    When these tears are gone, that will be
    The last of the woman in me. (*He exits.*)

KING: Let's follow him, dear wife.
    We'll try to make sure he's all right.

(*The* KING *and the* QUEEN *exit.*)

# Act 5

*Two gravediggers prepare the ground for Ophelia's funeral. Hamlet talks about how death treats everyone equally.*

*During the funeral, Hamlet and Laertes fight over who loved Ophelia more. Later, Hamlet tells Horatio about his experiences while at sea, on the way to England.*

*Hamlet and Laertes duel, with fatal results for them, the queen, and the king. Fortinbras returns from Poland and claims his place as the new king of Denmark.*

## Scene 1

*A graveyard. A* GRAVEDIGGER *and his* HELPER *enter.*

GRAVEDIGGER: Is this to be a
    Christian burial, in spite of being a suicide?

HELPER: Yes, or so I have heard.
    The coroner said it's a Christian burial.

GRAVEDIGGER: Perhaps it was not suicide.
    Or perhaps he is just looking the other way
    Because she was a gentlewoman.
    Who knows? And who cares?
    All I want is a drink! Why don't you go
    Down to the tavern and get us something?

(HELPER *exits.* GRAVEDIGGER *continues digging. As he digs, he sings.* HAMLET *and* HORATIO *enter.*)

HAMLET: Doesn't this fellow have any
    Feelings of sympathy for the dead?
    How can he sing while digging a grave?

HORATIO: He is so used to doing his job
   That he doesn't really think about it.

HAMLET: You're probably right.
   Only people who don't work much
   Have time for delicate feelings.

GRAVEDIGGER (*singing*):
   "But age with his stealing steps
   Has got me in his clutch.
   And soon will put me in the ground
   As if I had never been much."

(*He hits a skull with his shovel and throws it up
to the surface.*)

HAMLET: That skull had a tongue in it,
   And could sing once. How that gravedigger
   Throws it around as if it were nothing!
   (*He picks it up.*) This might be the head of
   A politician or a lord. And now he's just
   Food for worms. His jaw is gone,
   And he's been tossed about with a shovel.
   Were these bones born for no other reason
   Than to be used for playing games?
   My bones ache as I think about it.

GRAVEDIGGER (*singing*):
   "A pickax and a spade, a spade,
   Dig a deep hole for the latest guest.
   Get a burial sheet for the lovely maid
   She'll soon be here for her final rest."

(*He throws up a second skull.*)

HAMLET: There's another. Could that be
   The skull of a lawyer? Where are his

Arguments now, his cases, his evidence,
And all his tricks? Why does he allow this
Rude gravedigger to knock him about
With a dirty shovel? Shouldn't he accuse
The brute of assault? Hmm. This fellow
Might have been a great buyer of land.
Is this what he ends up with—
His fine head full of fine dirt?
His deeds and legal papers would hardly
Fit into this box. Must the buyer himself
Have no more room than this?

HORATIO: Not an inch more, my lord.

HAMLET (*to the* GRAVEDIGGER): My man,
Whose grave is this?

GRAVEDIGGER: Mine, sir. I am digging it.

HAMLET: What man are you digging it for?

GRAVEDIGGER: For no man, sir.

HAMLET: For what woman, then?

GRAVEDIGGER: For no woman, either.

HAMLET: Then who will be buried in it?

GRAVEDIGGER: One who was a woman,
But rest her soul, she's dead.

HAMLET: You are so careful with words!
How long have you been a gravedigger?

GRAVEDIGGER: I began on the day that our
Last King Hamlet defeated old Fortinbras,
30 years ago. It was the very day
That young Hamlet was born—he who
Went mad and was sent to England.

HAMLET: Why was he sent to England?

GRAVEDIGGER: Why, because he was mad.
 He shall get better there. Or, if he doesn't,
 It won't matter much.

HAMLET: Why?

GRAVEDIGGER: No one there will notice it.
 In England, everyone is as mad as he is.

HAMLET: Say, how long will a man
 Lie buried before he rots?

GRAVEDIGGER: Oh, eight or nine years.
 Here's a skull that has been in the earth
 For 23 years. (*He picks up a skull.*)
 He was certainly a joker!
 He poured some wine over my head once.
 This skull, sir, was Yorick's skull.
 He was the king's jester.

HAMLET: This? (*He takes the skull.*)

GRAVEDIGGER: That very one.

HAMLET: Alas, poor Yorick!
 I knew him, Horatio. He was a fellow
 Of infinite fun. He carried me on his back
 A thousand times. I hate to think of this!
 Here hung those lips that I kissed
 Too many times to count.
 Where are your jokes now, your tricks,
 Your songs, your flashes of merriment?
 Not one left to mock at your own grinning?
 Down-in-the-mouth, are you? Go to
 My lady's room right now. Tell her that
 No matter how much she paints her face,

She will end up like this.
Make her laugh at that!
Horatio, do you think Alexander the Great
Looked like this in the earth?

HORATIO: Just the same.

HAMLET: And smelled like this?

(*He throws down the skull.*)

HORATIO: Just the same, my lord.

HAMLET: Don't you find it interesting,
    Horatio, that the noble dust of Alexander
    Could end up as filling for a knot-hole?

HORATIO: You wonder too much, Hamlet.

HAMLET: But just think about it.
Alexander died, he was buried, and
He returned to dust. The dust is earth,
And from earth we get clay. Why shouldn't
Alexander's own clay be used to stop up
A hole in a beer-barrel?
The conquering Caesar, turned into clay,
Might plug a hole to keep the wind away.
Oh, that he who kept the world in fear
Might thus keep winter from coming near!
But that's enough for now. Look!
(*A* PRIEST, *the* KING, *the* QUEEN, LAERTES, *and*
LORDS *enter.* BEARERS *carry a coffin.*)
Who could be in the coffin?
And why are there so few mourners?
This suggests a suicide. It must have been
Someone of high rank.
Let's hide here and watch.

LAERTES: What other ceremonies
Will there be?

PRIEST: We have already done all we can
For her funeral ceremonies.

LAERTES: Lay her in the earth, then.
From her grave may violets grow.
I tell you, my sister is already in heaven.

HAMLET: What, the fair Ophelia?

QUEEN (*scattering flowers*):
Sweets to the sweet. Farewell.
I hoped that you would marry Hamlet.

I thought I would have decorated your
Bridal bed with flowers, sweet maid.
Instead, I spread them on your grave.

LAERTES: May countless woes fall on
The man who caused your madness.
Don't bury her yet! Wait until I have
Held her once more in my arms!
(LAERTES *leaps into the grave*.)
Now pile the earth on both of us!

HAMLET (*coming forward*): Who is this
That makes such a show of his grief?

LAERTES: Who is this
That comes uninvited?

HAMLET: This is I, Hamlet the Dane!

LAERTES: You monster!
You are responsible for her death!
(*They fight*.)

HAMLET: You're wrong about that!
Take your fingers from my throat!

KING (*to some* LORDS): Pull them apart!

HAMLET: Why, I'll fight him about this
Until the last moment of my life!
I loved Ophelia. Not even 40,000
Brothers could love her as much as I did.

KING: Oh, he is mad, Laertes.

HAMLET: Did you come to show your love
By leaping into her grave? Be buried alive
With her, and so will I! If you're going to
Rant and rave, I'll rant as loudly as you.

QUEEN: This is madness.

HAMLET: Laertes, why do you act like this?
 We have always been friends.
 But it is no matter.
 Let Hercules do what he may,
 The cat will mew,
 And the dog will have his day.

(HAMLET *exits*.)

KING: Good Horatio, look after him.
 (HORATIO *exits. To* LAERTES:)
 Be patient. Think about our talk last night.
 You'll soon have another chance to fight.

(*All exit*.)

# Scene 2

*Inside the castle walls.* HAMLET *and* HORATIO
*enter.*

HAMLET: I never finished telling you
 About what happened on the ship.
 We were on our way to England—
 Rosencrantz, Guildenstern, and I.
 In my heart there was a kind of fighting
 That kept me awake. On an impulse—
 And thank God for such impulses: this one
 Might have saved my life—I got up.
 I left my cabin, wrapping my sailor's coat
 Around me. I groped my way to them.
 I finally found them sleeping, and I stole
 Their packet of letters and papers.
 Back in my own room, my fears forgetting
 My manners, I opened their letters.

There I found a message from our king
To the king of England. As soon as he
Finished the letter, without even stopping
To sharpen the ax, the king of England
Was to have my head cut off!

HORATIO: I can hardly believe it!

HAMLET: Here's proof. Read it yourself.
Would you like to hear what I did?

HORATIO: Yes, I certainly would.

HAMLET: I sat down immediately
And wrote another letter. In it,
I ordered the king of England,
In the name of our "friendship,"
To put the bearers of the letter
To sudden death. They were not even
To have enough time to say any prayers.
Of course, I signed it with the name
Of my mother's husband. I had my father's
Official sealing ring in my bag.
It matches the present king's seal.
I folded up the new letter, sealed it,
And put it back where I had found it.
Rosencrantz and Guildenstern never even
Knew it had been missing.
The next day, the pirates attacked us.
You know the rest of the story.

HORATIO: Rosencrantz and Guildenstern
Went to their deaths?

HAMLET: Why, they loved their work.
They are not on my conscience.

If they hadn't been pandering to the king,
They would still be safe. When lesser men
Come between the swords of the mighty,
They take their own risks.

HORATIO: What kind of king do we have?

HAMLET: A villain and a murderer!
He killed my father, disgraced my mother,
And stood between me and the crown.
Then he tried to have me killed!
Wouldn't it be perfect if I could put an end
To him and all his evil?

HORATIO: He'll soon learn what happened
When the king of England gets your letter.

HAMLET: I'm sure he'll find out very soon.
But meanwhile, he won't suspect me.
It doesn't take long to end a man's life.
But I am very sorry, dear Horatio,
That I lost control of myself with Laertes.
I'll try to make it up to him.

(*A* MESSENGER *enters.*)

MESSENGER: My lord, I have a message
From the king. He wishes me to tell you
That he has placed a large bet on your skill.
As you no doubt already know,
Laertes has great skill with the sword.
The king has bet six fine horses
That you are even better than Laertes.
The exact bet was this: in 12 passes
Between you and Laertes, he wouldn't

Be able to hit you more than 3 times.
Laertes, on the other hand, says that
He will hit you 9 times out of 12.
The bet could be settled immediately
If you would accept the challenge.

HAMLET: Sir, here is my answer.
Let the swords be brought. I am willing.
If the king hasn't changed his mind,
I will win the bet for him if I can.
If not, I will gain nothing but my shame.

(MESSENGER *exits*.)

HORATIO: You will lose, my lord.

HAMLET: I do not think so. Since Laertes
Went to France, I have been practicing.
Even so, I feel a little uneasy about this.
But it is of no consequence.

HORATIO: If you have uneasy feelings,
Don't ignore them. I'll say you're ill.

HAMLET: Not at all. I don't pay attention
To omens and bad feelings.
Everything happens in its own time.
If death comes now, it won't come later.
If it doesn't come now, it will come later.
In any case, it will come sooner or later.
Being ready for it is all that counts.

(*The* KING, *the* QUEEN, LAERTES, LORDS, *and*
ATTENDANTS *carrying swords enter.*)

KING: Come, Hamlet, and shake hands
With Laertes. (HAMLET *does so.*)

HAMLET (*to* LAERTES): Forgive me, sir.
I have done you wrong. I am sure that
You've heard I haven't been myself lately.
I'm sorry if I offended you.

LAERTES: No offense was taken.

KING: Give them the swords.
Young Hamlet, you know the bet?

HAMLET: Very well, my lord.
You have bet on the weaker side.

LAERTES (*finding that he has not been given the poisoned sword*): This one is too heavy!
Let me have another one.

HAMLET: This one's fine for me!

(*They prepare to duel.* SERVANTS *enter with cups of wine.*)

KING: Set the wine on that table.
If Hamlet wins, I'll drink to his health!

HAMLET (*to* LAERTES): Come on, sir.

LAERTES (*to* HAMLET): Come on, my lord.

(*They begin their swordplay.* HAMLET *scores the first point.*)

KING: Good! I'll have a drink to that!
(*He drinks.*) Hamlet, have a drink yourself!
(*He secretly puts the poison into the cup and raises it as trumpets play.*)

HAMLET: I'll play this bout first.
Set it aside for a moment.

(*They continue their swordplay.*)

HAMLET: Another hit!

KING: I think Hamlet will win.

QUEEN: But he's out of shape
    And short of breath. Here, Hamlet,
    Take my handkerchief and wipe your brow.
    I'll drink to your good luck!

(*She picks up the poisoned cup.*)

KING: Gertrude, do not drink!

QUEEN: I shall, my lord, if you don't mind.

(*She drinks and offers the cup to* HAMLET.)

KING (*aside*): It is the poisoned cup.
    It is too late.

HAMLET: Not just yet, madam. Later.

LAERTES (*to the* KING): My lord,
    I'll hit him now.

KING: I don't think so.

LAERTES (*aside*): And yet it seems to go
    Against my conscience.

HAMLET: Come for the third bout, Laertes.
    You are wasting time. Come on!

LAERTES: All right!

(*They continue their swordplay. They fight
fiercely, and* LAERTES *wounds* HAMLET. *Continuing
to fight, they drop their weapons during a scuf-
fle. Each one accidentally picks up the other's
sword. Then* HAMLET *wounds* LAERTES *with the
poisoned sword. At the same time, the* QUEEN
*falls.*)

HORATIO: Both of them are bleeding!
   (*to* HAMLET) How are you, my lord?

HAMLET: How is the queen?

KING: She faints from seeing you bleed.

QUEEN: No, no, the drink, the drink!
   Oh, my dear Hamlet! The drink, the drink!
   I am poisoned. (*The* QUEEN *dies.*)

HAMLET: Oh, villainy! Stop everything!
   Lock the doors! Find the traitor!

LAERTES: It is here, Hamlet.
   You've been killed, and so have I.
   We have less than 30 minutes to live.
   The treacherous weapon is in your hand.
   The tip had no guard, and it was poisoned.
   Your mother is poisoned. I can say no more.
   The king—the king's to blame!

HAMLET: The point is poisoned?
   Then, poison, to your work!
   (HAMLET *stabs the* KING.) And just in case,
   You murderous Dane, finish this drink!
   Follow my mother! (*He forces the* KING *to
   drink, and the* KING *dies.*)

LAERTES: It is only fair. It was all his idea.
   Exchange forgiveness with me, Hamlet.
   I forgive you for my death and my father's.
   Forgive me for yours. (LAERTES *dies.*)

HAMLET: Heaven forgive you. I follow you.
   Unhappy queen, farewell!

I am dead, Horatio. You are alive.
Tell my story to those who don't know it.
(*A* MESSENGER enters, *with news that*
FORTINBRAS *returns in victory from Poland.*)
Oh, I die, Horatio. I won't live long enough
To see Fortinbras. But I predict that
he will become king of Denmark.
He has my dying vote. Tell him
(HAMLET *cannot finish the sentence*)—
The rest is silence.
(*The poison takes effect, and* HAMLET *dies.*)

HORATIO: There ends a noble life.
Good night, sweet prince,
May flights of angels sing you to your rest!

(*Sounds of marching are heard.* FORTINBRAS,
ENGLISH AMBASSADORS, *and* SOLDIERS *enter.*)

FORTINBRAS: What's all this?

HORATIO: What would you like to see?
If it's sorrow and woe, look no further.

FIRST AMBASSADOR: This is a dismal sight.
Our news from England comes too late.
The person who gave the order is dead.
Rosencrantz and Guildenstern are dead.
Now where will we get our thanks?

HORATIO (*pointing to the* KING):
Not from his mouth, even if
He could speak. He did not give the order.
I will tell you now what has happened here.

FORTINBRAS: Let us hear it right away.
I have some rights to this kingdom,
Which I shall now claim.

HORATIO: I shall speak about that, too.
But for now, let us honor these dead.

FORTINBRAS: Let four captains
Carry Hamlet like a soldier. For his funeral,
Let soldier's music and military salutes
Speak loudly for him. Raise the bodies.
A sight like this belongs on the battlefield.
Here, it seems very out of place.
Go, bid the soldiers shoot.

(*A salute of guns is fired. Drums beat. The
bodies are carried out. All exit.*)